# Canaanite Mythology

## Gods and Religion of Ancient Canaan

# Preface

Have you ever wondered about the gods and religion of ancient Canaan?

This book explores the history and beliefs of the Canaanites from their earliest recorded beginnings through to their absorption into the larger ancient Near Eastern religious and cultural traditions. In this easy-to-read and comprehensive guide, you will learn about the gods and goddesses of Canaanite mythology, as well as the religious beliefs and practices of the people.

# Table of Contents

# Introduction

Have you ever heard the stories of El and Anat, Baal and Asherah, Yamm and Mot, or Athirat and Yam? These are all characters from Canaanite mythology, an ancient religion that was once widespread in the Middle East. The Canaanites were a major Semitic-speaking civilization that inhabited the region between modern-day Israel, Lebanon, and Syria.

The Canaanite religion was a fascinating one. It included various gods and goddesses who were believed to be in charge of nature and the fate of people alike. Each deity had control over a different realm of life, which could range from fertility, farming, and abundance to war, weather, and other natural disasters. The stories associated with these gods taught lessons about righteousness and morality while guiding how to live a good life. Many aspects of Canaanite beliefs still influence modern practices in Middle Eastern countries today.

The history of Canaanite religion dates back to the Bronze Age, around 2000 BC. This era of great cultural exchange between different civilizations in the region likely influenced the development of Canaanite beliefs. Different gods and goddesses were added to their pantheon as time passed, with each deity representing certain aspects of life. With the rise of monotheism in the region, these polytheistic beliefs gradually faded away.

Today, we can still learn about the gods and goddesses of Canaanite mythology, their stories, and the practices that were associated with them. While many of the details have been lost to time, scholars have reconstructed much of the religion's cosmology by studying ancient texts and artifacts. Some dedicated researchers have even reconstructed a few of the rituals that were once practiced in honor of the gods and goddesses.

In this guide, we will explore the history, cosmology, and various gods and goddesses of Canaanite mythology. We'll also examine some of the religious beliefs and practices that were associated with the religion and how they may have shaped modern-day customs in the region. By the end of this book, you'll have a better understanding of the Canaanite religion and its impact on today's culture.

Contemplating the ancient gods and goddesses of the Canaanite religion can be a rewarding experience. Learning about their stories, symbols, and rituals will leave you with a newfound appreciation for the diversity of religious beliefs in our world. In the following pages, you'll find out more about this fascinating religion and the gods who once ruled over it. You'll also gain insight into how Canaanite culture has influenced our own beliefs and practices.

# Chapter 1:

## The History of Canaanite Religion

The Canaanite religion was a fascinating polytheistic religion that was once widely practiced by the ancient inhabitants of present-day areas in and around modern Israel. Historians believe a combination of environmental and spiritual forces led to the adoption of this belief system, with unique gods associated with different aspects of nature, including fire, rain, and fertility. Furthermore, features like temples and altars have been discovered among these cultures' ruins; evidence of long-running religious practices passed down from generation to generation.

While much about this ancient faith is lost to time, it remains an important part of our understanding of the region's history and its people. This chapter will explore the history of the Canaanite religion. It will discuss who practiced it, when and where it was practiced, and its basis and structure.

It will also compare the Canaanite religion to other ancient religions in the region and look at its connection to modern religions.

## The Canaanite Religion

The Canaanite religion was an ancient Semitic-speaking polytheistic religion that began as early as the 18th century BCE. Worshiped by the people of Canaan, many of the deities were inspired by local nature, with each one having a different role in their beliefs and customs. Although there isn't much knowledge about the specifics of their religion due to a lack of written evidence, insights can be gained through analysis of artifacts found throughout their settlements. The Canaanites believed in all kinds of spiritual rituals, offerings to their many gods, and festivals involving celebration or mourning periods. People would often flock to holy sites like temples to honor and worship whichever god they chose. This unique culture provides us with insight into a time long gone, making it an incredibly interesting topic to explore!

# The Practitioners of the Canaanite Religion

For those who don't know much about the Canaanite religion, it is crucial to understand its early practitioners. The Canaanites campaigned all around the Mediterranean, building empires and engaging in plenty of trade. These groups of people began embracing the Canaanite religion, which had a host of gods and goddesses to worship. The early Canaanites believed in worshiping their deities by engaging in acts like sacrifice and building temples to honor them. It was an intricate religion with its own mythology and astrology. Along with this, holy sites throughout their territory played an integral part in their beliefs and practices. Although many modern religions have evolved from these ancient beliefs, it's clear that early practitioners of the Canaanite religion left a lasting impact on generations to come.

## The Origins of the Canaanite Religion

The Canaanite religion is one of the oldest known religions, with many scholars tracing its origins back to the early Bronze Age. Like many other ancient religions, it focused heavily on nature and the worship of gods who controlled natural elements like water and storms. These gods have been identified in artifacts from local cultures around the Mediterranean Sea and were likely from many different beliefs from before recorded history. The evolution of this faith saw its pantheon of deities formed around ancestral gods like El and Asherah, leading to the development of concepts like kingship, justice, fertility, and love that remain present in Canaanite beliefs today.

## The Structure of the Canaanite Pantheon

The pantheon of ancient Canaanites was an incredibly complex structure composed of various gods and goddesses. With over 200 deities in each regional pantheon, the diversity they displayed reflects the ingenuity and creativity of this ancient civilization. For instance, many scholars identify Anat and Astarte as the two most important female divinities in the entire pantheon, representing sexual energy and sovereignty. El was arguably the chief deity in many regions, ruling over nature and creation alongside his consort Asherah.

Baal was initially a singular deity who later transformed into a composite god, taking on many different aspects within each region's pantheon. Interestingly, all these deities had shrines, rituals, symbols, and stories that further embodied their importance and that of their respective worshippers. All in all, the structure of the Canaanite pantheon was complex yet adaptive enough to tackle any changes occurring through time without disrupting its strength or foundation.

## The Supreme God

Exploring the ancient cultural pantheons of the world can be an exciting journey and a wonderful way to learn more about past people and their spiritual practices. If you take a look at the ancient Canaanite culture, you will find that their spiritual tradition revolves around the supreme god El, who was at the top of their hierarchical pantheon structure. For example, El allowed many deities known as Baals to live alongside him and work together to fulfill various important roles in creating or governing the universe. While El is considered the oldest member of this pantheon with few specific attributes, he serves as an essential example of unity between differing divine entities that created a strong spiritual identity throughout Canaanite regions long ago.

## Primary Gods

It's no secret that the Canaanite pantheon is filled with a fascinating array of powerful primary gods. Five main gods are at the top, each of them representing different elemental aspects and playing an integral role in the functioning universe. El, the head of the group is the most significant one of all. He is the fatherly ruler who presides over storms, rain, and fertility. Next comes Baal, the God of storm and weather. He ensures that plants grow, producing food for animals and people alike. Asherah is the goddess of fertility, while Anat is the goddess of war and fertility at once, who encompasses concepts such as love and violence. Finally, there's Yarikh, the God of harvest and fruitfulness. He protects crops from harm during summer months for a successful harvest. These five primary gods keep Canaanite life vibrant and provide for people in many ways.

## Minor Deities

The Canaanite pantheon is an intriguing structure that reflects their ancient culture and values. It consists of a foremost sovereign lord of the gods and a collection of minor deities representing natural forces like fertility, harvest, and rain. These deities are believed to be responsible for the success of everyday life, from individual households to entire nations. Many recognizable characters from literature and mythology formed part of this pantheon. Dagon, Tammuz, and Moloch were all part of the structure. Minor gods were given human-like attributes to illustrate their power over their domains. That made them much easier to understand and relate to. A fascinating detail about these minor gods was that they could also be localized by different religious communities around Canaan and incorporated into specific cults when they believed they needed more personalized guidance. All in all, this complex network offered worshippers protection and insight into many aspects of life.

## Comparison to Other Religions

The Canaanite religion is incredibly unique and stands out from many other belief systems. It is a polytheistic faith, which makes it quite different from monotheistic religions like Christianity and Islam. At its core, the religion focuses on the worship of El, considered the father figure of numerous gods in the Pantheon. He presides over the Assembly of Gods and oversees a variety of rituals involving sacrifices to honor these celestial beings. Different communities had different customs depending on their environment and beliefs, but most featured offerings to forest spirits or ancestor idols as part of their practice. The Canaanites also held strong ideas regarding cosmic justice that no person will reap what they do not sow; wrongdoers will be punished while righteous people are rewarded in kind. Ultimately, while similar in structure to other faiths, the Canaanite religion's combination of spirituality, magical taboos, and laws provide a fascinating window into mankind's religious past.

## Mesopotamian Religion

The comparison of the Canaanite religion to the Mesopotamian religion reveals an interesting contrast, with different practices and beliefs on either side. On the one hand, the Canaanites believed in a pantheon of gods, each with their areas of influence, while on the other hand, the Mesopotamians held largely to a single chief god, from whom all others derived their power. Further, while Mesopotamian worship emphasized sacrifice to appease the gods and ensure divine favor, Canaanite ritual practices were much more varied, ranging from offerings to holy music. Both religions held similar views on who controlled certain realms. For example, both saw Utu/Shamash as presiding over justice, but these two ancient faiths could not be more different when it came to day-to-day life and practice.

## Greek and Roman Religions

Both Ancient Canaanite and Greek/Roman religions are incredibly fascinating and complex, containing many interesting similarities and points of contrast. For instance, a characteristic shared by both the Canaanite religion and Greek/Roman religions is the notion of divine intervention in human affairs to influence or guide them in specific ways. Additionally, both groups had similar gods. Canaanite gods such as El, Baal, and Anat often found similar counterparts among gods in the Greek and Roman pantheons.

On the other hand, differences between the Canaanite tradition and those practiced by Greeks and Romans were very pronounced. While polytheism pervaded throughout Ancient Greece or Rome's religious affairs, some Orthodox Canaanites only idolized a single god. Moreover, while Ancient Greeks/Romans frequently built temples devoted to one particular deity or another, there appears to be little evidence that the land-bound Canaanites built temples at all. All in all, it can be seen that these ancient religious cultures each bore their unique nuances without failing to share some commonalities across their societies.

## Judaism

The similarities between the Canaanite religion and Judaism can be found in their shared concepts of personal morality. In both religions, the highest authority is God, and believers must uphold the moral standards set within their faiths. Both religions also embrace prayer as a significant part of their practices, although it's believed that the language used might differ between the two. While there are some aspects of Jewish law that Canaanites did not observe, like keeping kosher and wearing hats to cover one's head during prayer. Overall, many traditions with strong ethical themes remain consistent across both religious practices. It would appear that these two faiths have intertwined over centuries of influence, leaving us with much to appreciate in terms of cultural diversity today.

## Connection to Modern Religions

The connection between the Canaanite religion and modern religions is an incredibly fascinating subject. While it's impossible to determine exactly how much of the Canaanite religion's elements have been passed down to us, we do know that many religious traditions and practices today are reminiscent of the gods and goddesses of ancient mythology. For example, some biblical scholars believe that one of the most worshiped Hebrew gods, Yahweh, was modeled after El, a war god in Canaanite mythology. It is these kinds of connections that keep our modern faiths alive and are a testament to their strength across centuries.

## Christianity

Christianity is one of the world's most widely practiced religions; its roots can be traced back to the Canaanites of thousands of years ago. The awe-inspiring accounts of God's power in his relationships with humans that are found throughout the Old Testament emerged from stories and beliefs formulated by the ancient Canaanites. Many believe that although Jesus wasn't born until well after their time, he incorporated various aspects of their religion into teachings himself. His account of creation, his mission on Earth, and even his moral code were heavily influenced by this faith tradition. The message spread by Jesus can still be found alive and well today but is rooted in an old and treasured people who held a unique relationship with an ever-present divinity.

## Islam

The connection of the Canaanite religion to Islam is nothing short of intriguing. Although not an identical match, there are several similarities between the two religions, most notably centered on mythology and icons. It is believed that these ancient people shared deities like Banal, El, and Asherah, which parallels the Islamic mention of Allah and their devotion to one God. In exploring both texts further, it can be seen that many archetypal characters in each faith were inspired by the earlier Canaanite stories, such as likening Moses to Gilgamesh from Mesopotamian folklore. Although Islam does maintain its belief system and practices that originated long after the Canaanite religion declined, it does offer many hints of familiarity for those who are paying attention.

## Neo-Paganism

It is interesting to see how certain religions, such as the Canaanite religion, have continuously been embraced and reinterpreted by Neo-pagans over the centuries. From honoring nature and personal spirituality to a focus on magic and personal well-being, much of the ancient mysticism that Canaanites practiced is alive and well in Neo-paganism today. To those who believe in either one or both religions, it can be a source of comfort to know that these traditions have survived so long, remaining connected even after so much time, continuing to provide an emotional connection to our shared humanity.

The Canaanite religion is a fascinating piece of ancient history that remains relevant today, influencing modern religions and traditions alike. From providing the foundation for Christianity and Islam to inspiring Neopaganism, this ancient faith tradition has seen its influence span centuries, connecting us all with something profoundly human. Though scarce in literary sources, the Canaanite religion remains an important reminder of our shared past and offers a unique perspective on humanity's never-ending quest for meaning and understanding. We honor the Canaanites for their impact on our collective spiritual journey, allowing us to glimpse an ancient world of gods and goddesses and to find our paths in the present.

# Chapter 2:

## Canaanite Cosmology

The Canaanite religion is quite interesting for many people because it was a polytheistic religion that existed thousands of years ago in ancient Palestine and Syria. It remains popular today due to its prevalence in the book of Genesis with characters such as Noah, Abraham, and Lot. Ancient texts have outlined some of the most important elements of this religion, including ancestor worship and ritual purification. As many ancient religions do, much of the power wielded was through the priesthood. There are records suggesting their practices included divination, animal sacrifice, and even possibly human sacrifice.

Today, we can look back on these fascinating practices and consider how drastically different religions in those regions have become over time, making the Canaanite religion even more historically remarkable. This chapter will explore the cosmology of the Canaanites and its various aspects, including their creation story and explanation of the pantheon of gods. The narrative will also delve into the mythology associated with this religion, such as the Twin Mountains Targhizizi and Tharumagi protecting the Earth, the Baal Cycle, and Elohim Cycle. Additionally, the afterlife will be explored with a look at the Ugarit underworld, heaven, and hell, as well as the judgment of the dead, resurrection, and reincarnation.

## Creation Story

The Canaanite religion's narrative is fascinating, and it starts with an incredibly unique story of creation. The Ugaritic Texts explain this mysterious first chapter in the history of Canaanite belief and detail many other aspects, including their gods and goddesses. What's special about these texts is that they take on a plethora of forms, from prose to poetry. It's amazing to think that ancient literature has survived to this day so we can piece together something of the past and make it relevant for today. Learning more about the Canaanite religion helps us gain a better appreciation for what makes up the world around us.

According to this tale, their god El led the other gods to create a vast cosmic ocean which they filled with all kinds of creatures. Then El separated the sky, sea, and land and set the world in its place. He created the two great mountains of Targhizizi and Tharumagi to bind the Earth in place. El then appointed his son, Baal, to be the ruler of the world and its creatures.

## Overview of the Pantheon

The Canaanite pantheon encompasses a plethora of ancient gods and goddesses built around the worship of Baal. Worship of these varied deities had deep roots throughout Levantine culture, as evidenced by many artifacts and evidence created thousands of years ago. While there was much overlap between different pantheons in the region, the unique deities found in the Canaanite religion have been revered for centuries. Each deity inhabited a specific role, with primary gods like Baal responsible for fertility and El for kingship. Others played more mischievous roles, like Amen, around whom tales were spun about his trickery and mischief. Ultimately, viewing the larger picture gives us insight into many aspects of life from that era that are still relevant today.

## Religious Texts

Religions have always inspired a sense of wonder, reverence, and awe. Ancient Canaan was no exception to this. They had a vast pantheon that included many gods and goddesses. The religious texts associated with the Canaanite pantheon provide an incredible insight into their spiritual beliefs, displaying their devotion to the divine as well as their elaborate rituals. From prayers for assistance and protection to magical incantations for success in life, these religious texts are fascinating windows into the ancient culture and beliefs of the people of Canaan. A few of these writings have even been preserved in museum collections allowing us access to parts of cultures once thought lost in antiquity!

Some of the most significant religious texts associated with the Canaanite religion include the Baal Cycle, Elohim Cycle, and Atrahasis Epic. These epics serve to educate, entertain, and provide instruction from the gods. They are filled with stories of sacrifice and battle, providing us a glimpse into the past, where we find ancient gods and goddesses locked in conflict to maintain order amongst humans.

## Mythology

The Canaanite mythology is an incredible and vibrant tradition, containing stories and characters full of power and wit. It all began in the distant past, within the ancient Near East amongst the ancient Canaanite people. From this ancient culture emerges stories of love, power, and struggle that take us through enchanted worlds with beguiling characters who capture our attention and arouse our imaginations. Some of the most recognized figures from this illustrious tradition are Baal, Astarte, and El, but these are only scratching the surface as there are many more extraordinary tales to be told!

## Twin Mountains

The twin Mountains have an important place in Canaanite mythology. According to ancient myths, Rhea, Zeus's mother, used the two mountains to hide her infant son from his father, who was determined to swallow his children. This myth is believed to stem from the eons-long rivalry between tribes, each claiming sacredness over one or other of the twin peaks. Historians believe they were created in the early Bronze Age as a symbol of cooperation between local clans and tribes. Even today, locals still make pilgrimages to both peaks, telling stories of their battle-toughened heroes who defended the Twin Mountains through generations. Perhaps this is why some regard the Twin Mountains as places full of blessings, good luck, and a reminder that with unity comes strength!

## Baal Cycle

The Baal Cycle is one of the fascinating aspects of Canaanite mythology. It's filled with brilliant characters, entertaining stories, and colorful symbolism that can still be studied today. In this rich saga, Baal is the central figure who fought to recapture from Mot, the god of death, the divine throne of El that he believed was rightfully his. Along with his consort, Anath, Baal fought many powerful battles, both physical and metaphorical, to ensure that his descendants would not have eternal servitude under Mot. Ultimately, what remains most memorable is the way this mythology speaks to humanity's eternal duality between life and death.

## Elohim Cycle

The Elohim Cycle is an integral part of ancient Canaanite mythology, providing great insight into the beliefs and behaviors of the cultures from which it originated. This cycle presents us with a powerful set of adventures and gods that offer many parallels to our modern world. Elohim, one of the principal figures, is presented as an omnipotent creator and protector of humanity, a figure we can still see reflected in the leaders we look up to today. Further on, Elohim's progeny carry out disputes against each other that bring this mythical narrative to life, allowing us to glimpse at different aspects of humanity through a combination of gods and humans. Exploring this captivating cycle in depth provides unmatched insight into our past, offering us clues to understand how we behave today.

## Origin of Mankind

The Canaanite mythology has grown to be one of the fascinating theories of the origin of mankind.

According to this ancient belief, humans were created from clay by a divine being known as El. In ancient texts, it is stated that he made man and woman companions to each other for comfort and reproduction. This theory also explains why death entered the world. El marks man's time upon Earth when he breathes life into him but warns that he will eventually return to dust. This idea was very popular in the early days and may have even inspired later religious beliefs. It can be difficult to trace its origins since many of these stories were shared orally among elders before they eventually found their way into more permanent written form; however, discovering them still provides an exciting glimpse of a society whose beliefs are so different from what we know today.

## Garden of Eden

Tucked away amidst the annals of ancient Canaanite mythology, one can find the fascinating tale of the Garden of Eden. This story entwines sacredness and divinity with beautiful imagery while also providing a warning to man against arrogance and pride. In this legend, Eden is a lush paradise located in a great divine tree that grows up from one of four rivers. This legend has been around for centuries, remaining relevant even to this day due to its timeless themes and moral truths. It speaks to our shared longing for harmony with nature and an acceptance of our mortality, enduring messages that linger in the minds of many people today.

## The Great Flood

The Great Flood is an integral part of Canaanite mythology, which tells the story of the gods using their power to bring a great flood to Earth to annihilate those they deem worthy of destruction. It is said that the great god Yaw was angry with mankind for not adhering to their laws, so he unleashed a catastrophic flood that swept away and obliterated many cities and civilizations. Although this myth has been echoed throughout several religions and cultures, scholars are still debating its origin and how much truth lies within it. Whether you take it as literal fact or simply an allegory, the narrative of The Great Flood is truly captivating and fascinating to explore.

## Tower Of Babel

Everyone's heard the story of Babel and how humanity tried to build a tower so tall that it could reach heaven, only to be foiled by God and get scattered around the world and given different languages. Did you know that that story is part of ancient Canaanite mythology? In this tale, humanity tries to take control away from their gods, the sky-god Baal and the Lord Asherah but fails tragically. The dream of a place where everyone could understand each other still has not come true, yet this ancient fable serves as a reminder that mankind can never truly grasp the ways of gods. What started as an attempt at reaching divinity has now become a universal warning not to strive too high without proper respect for forces beyond our understanding.

## Destruction of Sodom and Gomorrah

The legendary story of the destruction of Sodom and Gomorrah is featured prominently in Canaanite mythology. The myth recounts the tale of two cities filled with immorality and depravity that were destroyed by God. Despite society's claim to modernity, connections to this ancient story can still be found in today's literature and media. It serves as a warning for any who may transgress against God's commands. A fitting example of this is celebrated American author Nathaniel Hawthorn's work "The Scarlet Letter," where a young woman is forced to wear a physical badge of her sins and forever be condemned to suffering amidst her peers. Though Ancient Canaanite tales are not clear-cut reminders of living one's life upright anymore, they still offer unique perspectives on how generations since have thought about sin and morality.

## Abrahamic Covenant

The Abrahamic Covenant, found in the Bible's Old Testament, is an interesting legacy of Canaanite mythology. This mythology appears to be based on a covenant established between God and Abraham that was passed through generations in Abraham's descent. In this covenant, God promised Abraham land and that he would have a lot of descendants. While very similar to the story of Noah's Ark, the Abrahamic Covenant has a unique importance to many cultures around the world. The impact it has had on multiple religious groups is simply beautiful.

The idea that God made a pact with an individual human being was revolutionary at the time it was recorded and continues to be a powerful reminder to many people today.

## Exodus

The Canaanite mythology, recorded in the Bible's book of Exodus, is truly a fascinating story. It tells of a great exodus where Moses led the Hebrew people out of slavery in Egypt and made their way across the Red Sea. This pilgrimage was more than just a way of escape; it symbolized Hebrew freedom and redemption, something deeply rooted within their spiritual faith. Much like many other ancient civilizations, Egyptians viewed natural occurrences and disasters as direct interventions from their gods. In the case of Exodus, these tribulations became powerful symbols of both God's mighty power as well as god's justice. The account of this mass escape proved an invaluable source of insight into many aspects of Canaanite culture, including its language and religious practices. Even today, scholars continue to uncover the deeper meaning behind these captivating texts.

# Afterlife

In Canaanite mythology, the afterlife is a unique and fascinating concept. The religion envisioned many gods in the heavens and underworlds as well as a mysterious place between them. According to beliefs, one's soul could either be sent directly to heaven or wander in both realms until it could eventually reach paradise. Devotees believed that no matter the circumstances, their souls would find their way to the highest level of existence available after death. The idea of an afterlife provided believers with a sense of hope and peace of mind for their eternal journey to the gods.

# Ugarit Underworld

Ugarit Underworld is a forgotten world of Canaanite mythology. It was a mysterious locale where the dead dwelled, located beyond the mortal realm. In Ugarit, gods and goddesses interacted to keep a balance between the living and the dead. Stories from this era describe deities who guarded entrances and exits between life and death with their watchful eyes. Although much about this mythological underworld remains shrouded in secrets, it continues to pique modern-day curiosities about gods, goddesses, mortality, and what truly lies in our afterlife. With ancient creatures like Mot's ship of death promising an advisory journey towards the afterlife, the legend of Ugarit Underworld offers a captivating peek into the beliefs and spiritual practices of these long-lost people.

## Heaven and Hell

In Canaanite mythology, heaven and hell were commonly thought of as separate realms that people could go to depending on their life on Earth. Heaven was often described as a place of beauty filled with lush gardens, while hell was often depicted as a dark netherworld. It's no surprise that heaven is believed to be the ultimate reward for a good life, while hell is seen as the punishment for leading an immoral life, according to some beliefs. The most interesting aspect of this mythos is that it suggests people can avoid going to hell by simply leading a good life. Altogether, the Canaanite mythology gives us an interesting perspective on what our rewards or punishments are when this physical world comes to an end.

## Judgment of the Dead

The Canaanite mythology includes a unique belief in the afterlife called Judgment of the Dead. According to their beliefs, upon death, an individual's soul traveled to a well in El-Akha, where gods would determine their fate for eternity. It was believed that those who lived an honorable life were allowed to ascend to the high heavens and dwell with the gods, while those who transgressed were forced into servitude in the underworld. This mythology of judgment held people accountable for their actions during life on Earth and served as a reminder not to lead an unworthy existence or else face eternal sacrifice.

Canaanite mythology is rich and diverse in its beliefs and stories. Creation, afterlife, Ugarit underworld, heaven and hell, and Judgment of the Dead are just a few of the topics explored in this captivating mythology. Its lessons have been passed down through generations and continue to influence our perceptions of the world around us. Whether it's to provide a sense of hope or to warn us against immoral behavior, Canaanite mythology has something to offer us all. Ultimately, this ancient mythology can help guide us closer to understanding ourselves and the world we live in.

# Chapter 3:

---

# Gods of Canaanite Mythology

Canaanite mythology hails from the ancient Levant, a region in and around present-day Israel that was home to several Bronze Age cultures and civilizations. This mythology includes an array of gods, goddesses, and other supernatural entities who interacted with humans in various ways. From the sky god Baal to the sea god Dagon, each of these deities had their own stories, beliefs, and powers. Each of them also had its symbols and correspondences related to them and signs of power. In this chapter, we will explore the gods of Canaanite mythology, their names, stories, and myths, where and how they were worshiped, symbols and correspondences related to them, and signs of their power.

## Types of Gods in Canaanite Mythology

The gods in Canaanite mythology can be divided into two categories: Elohim and Baalim. The Elohim were the gods of fertility, agriculture, and abundance, while the Baalim were the warriors and protectors of their people. The major gods were the most powerful deities in the pantheon, such as El, Baal, Anat, Asherah, and Dagon. They each had a deep influence on the lives of humans and were worshiped widely across Canaanite culture. The minor gods were lesser gods and goddesses who were usually connected to one of the major gods or who had a smaller area of influence.

## Baal

Baal was the chief god of Canaanite mythology. He was a sky god who controlled the rain and storms and was associated with fertility, agriculture, and warfare. He was often represented by a bull. Baal's name means "master" or "lord," and he was believed to be the lord of the divine council.

### Stories and Myths

Stories about Baal described him as a powerful warrior who fought against chaos and monsters, such as the sea dragon Yamm, the death god Mot, and the storm god Lotan. In one story, Baal defeats

Yamm in a battle for control of the sea and then becomes the ruler of the universe.

## Worship

In Canaanite culture, Baal was widely worshiped in temples and shrines across the region. He was often invoked in times of drought and famine when his power over rain and storms could bring relief to the people.

## Symbols and Correspondences

The bull was the primary symbol of Baal, and it was believed to be his sacred animal. Other symbols associated with him included the sun, lightning, and fire. He was often associated with the god El, who was believed to be his father, as well as the goddess Anat, who was believed to be his sister and consort.

## Signs of Power

Baal's power was displayed in his ability to control the weather and bring fertility, abundance, and protection to the people. He could also manipulate fire and lightning and was often associated with the sun. The bull was a sign of his power, and he could take on its form in battle.

## Dagon

Dagon was the god of the sea in Canaanite mythology. He was born from chaos and associated with fertility, abundance, and protection. A fish or a merman-like figure usually represented him. His name means "grain" or "grain god," and he was believed to be the giver of life and fertility.

## Stories and Myths

Stories about Dagon described him as the ruler of the sea and the protector of fishermen. He defeated Lotan, the seven-headed sea serpent, and controlled the waters of the Mediterranean Sea. He was also associated with the fertility god Baal and was believed to be one of his sons.

## Worship

Dagon was widely worshiped in coastal cities and fishing villages across Canaanite culture. He was often invoked for protection on the sea and in times of famine.

## Symbols and Correspondences

The fish or merman was the primary symbol of Dagon, and it was his sacred animal. Other symbols associated with him included the moon, stars, and dolphins. He was often associated with Baal and Anat, who were believed to be his father and mother.

## Signs of Power

Dagon's power was displayed in his ability to control the sea and bring abundance and protection to fishermen. He could also manipulate the weather and was often associated with storms, rain, and fog. The fish or merman was a sign of his power, and he could take on its form in battle.

# El

El was the father of the gods in Canaanite mythology. He was a sky god who controlled the rain and storms and was associated with justice, wisdom, and fertility. He was usually represented by a bull or an eagle. His name means "god" or "lord," and he was believed to be the creator of the universe.

## Stories and Myths

Stories about El described him as a wise and just ruler of the gods. He was seen as a father figure to the other gods and often acted as an intermediary between them and humans. He was also associated with the fertility god Baal and the goddess Anat, who were believed to be his children.

## Worship

El was widely worshiped in temples and shrines across Canaanite culture. He was often invoked for protection, justice, and blessings of fertility and abundance. Some scholars believe that he was the original Canaanite supreme god before Baal took over the role.

## Symbols and Correspondences

The bull and eagle were the primary symbols of El, and they were his sacred animals. Other symbols associated with him included the sun, lightning, and stars. He was often associated with Baal and Anat, who were believed to be his children.

## Signs of Power

El's power was displayed in his ability to control the sky and bring justice, protection, and fertility to the people. He could also manipulate lightning and storms and was often associated with the sun. The bull and eagle were signs of his power, and he could take on their forms in battle. He was seen as the most powerful of all the gods.

# Mot

Mot was the god of death in Canaanite mythology. He was a destructive force associated with decay and chaos, and a dragon or a serpent usually represented him. His name means "death" or "that which brings death."

## Stories and Myths

Stories about Mot described him as a powerful and destructive force that could bring death and destruction. He was the ultimate enemy of Baal, and the two clashed in a great battle at the end of time. He was often associated with El and Anat, who were believed to be his parents.

## Worship

Mot was sometimes worshiped in temples and shrines, though he was seen as a destructive force, and there were not many people who wished to appease him. He was usually invoked in times of war or great danger when people believed his power could be beneficial.

## Symbols and Correspondences

The dragon or serpent was the primary symbol of Mot, and it was his sacred animal. Other symbols associated with him included fire, darkness, death, and destruction. He was often associated with El and Anat, who were believed to be his parents.

## Signs of Power

Mot's power was displayed in his ability to bring death and destruction. He could control the forces of chaos and decay and be often associated with storms, fire, and darkness. The dragon or serpent was a sign of his power, and he could take on its form in battle. He was seen as the ultimate enemy of Baal and all that was good.

# Aglibol

Aglibol was the god of the moon in Canaanite mythology. He was a protective and benevolent force associated with light, celestial knowledge, and the night sky. He was usually represented by a crescent moon. His name means "protector of the city," and he was believed to be the guardian of ancient cities and towns.

## Stories and Myths

Stories about Aglibol described him as a protective god who watched over the people and guided them in times of darkness. He was often associated with El and Anat, who were believed to be his parents. He had the power to bring light and knowledge to humans and was seen as a symbol of wisdom and guidance.

## Worship

Aglibol was widely worshiped in temples and shrines across Canaanite culture. He was often invoked for protection, guidance, and blessings of knowledge and wisdom. He was also associated with fertility and abundance and was seen as a symbol of hope in dark times.

## Symbols and Correspondences

The crescent moon was the primary symbol of Aglibol, and his sacred animal was the cow. Other symbols associated with him included stars, night skies, and knowledge. The moon was seen as a symbol of wisdom and guidance and believed to be connected to Aglibol.

## Signs of Power

Aglibol's power was displayed in his ability to bring light and knowledge to humans. He could watch over the people and provide them with guidance and protection. He was also associated with fertility and abundance, and he could bring blessings of abundance to those who invoked him. The crescent moon and cow were symbols of his power, and he could take on their forms in battle.

Canaanite mythology is filled with gods that are both powerful and benevolent. Each god has their symbols, correspondences, stories, and myths that describe its behavior and power. Dagon, Mot, and

Aglibol are just a few of the gods in Canaanite mythology. Each of these gods represents a different aspect of life and is an important part of mythology and culture. From protection to destruction, these gods show us the power of faith and belief in a higher power. Worship of these gods was widespread in Canaanite culture, and they were often invoked for protection, guidance, and blessings. Understanding the gods of Canaanite mythology gives us a glimpse into how this ancient culture viewed the world and its place in it.

# Chapter 4:

## Goddesses of Canaanite Mythology

The goddesses of Canaanite mythology have been venerated for many centuries, with their powerful and influential representations still resonating powerfully thousands of years later. Amongst the best-known are Asherah, the creator goddess and consort of El, and Anat, the warrior daughter of Baal Hadad. The goddesses upheld a variety of roles within these stories. Some were protectors, warriors, and others could be unpredictable or even dark, all etched into the memory of those that came before us.

Despite their varied characters, one thing was constant. Each held an important place in Canaanite mythology, which continues to influence beliefs until this day. This chapter will explore the stories, myths, and worship of the goddesses significant to Canaanite mythology and how they are represented. It will also discuss their symbolism, power, and the type of goddesses they were. By exploring these topics, it can be seen how the influence of Canaanite mythology continues to shape today's beliefs.

## Anat

Anat is the ancient Canaanite goddess of warfare and love, with a name that relates to 'task' or 'work.' She was deeply loved by her people, who told many stories and myths about her. Selected warriors gathered to worship her courage and strength through ritual ceremonies, either at temples or in secret circles outdoors. The image of Anat often featured symbols such as axes which were thought to belong to her powerful domains that included war, protection, and hunting. People believed that when invoking Anat's power, a person could be gifted with ferocity and victory on the battlefield. Thus, she is an example of an armed goddess-type deity working for humanity's higher causes, proving that although fierce and seemingly violent, she ultimately comes bearing gifts of courage and strength.

# Asherah

Asherah, a Canaanite goddess associated with fertility and motherhood, is an enduring part of ancient mythology and still carries relevance in today's society. Her name derives from the Semitic root 'ashr' and holds many possible meanings, such as "she who walks in the sea," "the trunk of the tree of life," or "she who creates through shifting ."With these roots in mind, it is easy to see why she was revered as a great source of power for many ancient people. The stories and myths that surround her are still diverse and creative after thousands of years. From legends about how she shaped the land to ritualistic worship practices involving pulling down stars from the Heavens themselves, it's no wonder why Asherah has been remembered for so long.

She is also known for being swift and generous, rewarding those who respect her divine power. In many rituals and ceremonies, she used symbols like cedar trees and correspondences with elements like fire to remind worshippers of her grace. Overall, Asherah stands out compared to other goddesses due to her powerful ability to offer protection, creation, and abundance to believers. For this reason, by looking back at the mighty deeds that are attributed to this deity, one can gain a sense of hope in our modern times.

## Astarte

Astarte, also known as Ashtoreth, was an ancient goddess featured in Canaanite mythology. Derived from the Semitic word for the goddess of fertility and war, 'Astarte' manifests two prominent characteristics, including motherly love and incredible strength. According to mythologies, Astarte had multiple lovers and children with powerful attributes. She was worshiped throughout the Middle East and helped promote fertility among her followers, though not always with benevolent consequences. In ceremonies, Astarte was revered with symbols such as eggs, fish, lions, and doves; essences such as myrrh; and acts of fire dance. Her role as a mother-warrior deity is echoed in many subsequent religions' figures of femininity across time. Astarte was one of the most powerful goddesses due to her representation of both protection and destruction while maintaining an ability to nurture life in society.

## Baalat

Baalat is an incredibly interesting goddess from Canaanite mythology and deserves more attention than she usually receives. Her name translates to 'Lady,' and many believe that she is the female counterpart to Baal, the supreme god of fertility. Legends about her are plentiful, describing her as a powerful deity who was worshiped for protection against chaos and evil. Those close to her found strength and healing in the presence of the goddess of brides, mistress of the gods, mother, and lover. Despite not being widely known among non-pagans, she has been given a variety of symbols associated with divinity, such as sacred cities, thrones, and lions. Furthermore, variations on fire and oil offerings have long been used in rituals to honor her spirit guides. To top it off, this alluring matron always protects what she loves with fierce devotion, making her a type of witch goddess who should never be underestimated.

## Eshmun

Eshmun is a popular figure in Canaanite mythology. Her name is thought to mean "sixth" and may refer to the sixth child of Baal and Anath. She's one of the most beloved goddesses in mythology, as her stories and myths are full of wonder and awe-inspiring feats. Most notably, Eshmun was worshiped for her healing powers. She was revered for her ability to treat any sickness, physical or spiritual. Besides being a patron of healing, she's also seen as an embodiment of nature, fertility, and femininity, attributes which were important to early cult followers. Along with her association with nature came various symbols, such as cornucopias, pomegranates, and snakes. As a chthonic goddess, one that connected the spiritual realm with the natural world, she represents very special powers that unite both realms harmoniously.

## Kothar-Wa-Khasis

Kothar-Wa-Khasis is a goddess in ancient Canaanite mythology. This majestic figure was very important to her people, and she was known among them as the 'Skillful One,' which aptly describes her power and abilities. In stories from this time, we learn that Kothar-Wa-Khasis had dominion over magic and even humans, according to some sources. She was extremely well respected by her followers and invoked for almost any blessing or favor needed for success. Representations of Kothar-Wa-Khasis often included lotus flowers, tools, the moon or stars, and items of power within the Canaanite myths associated with creation and strength. As a nature goddess in mythology, she can help and protect those seeking out her presence. A complex mixture of intimidating yet inviting energy pulsed around this beloved goddess.

## Shapash

Shapash, an ancient goddess of Canaanite mythology, has a fascinating history and provides colorful insights into the past. Though her exact name and meaning are somewhat debated, it is believed that Shapash comes from the ancient Semitic word for "light" or "torch," which may have been linked to her role as a bringer of justice and clarity. Beyond this, though, many stories or myths were created around Shapash over time, creating an interesting picture of her power and the symbolism she may have taken on during her worship.

Shapash was known as a type of sun goddess associated with fertility, metaphorical heat, spiritual discernment, and even death. Her symbols are thought to include spirals and wheels, specifically bovine horns, in correspondence with various animals which she may have had dominion over. Overall, while we can never know exactly how this ancient Canaanite deity was viewed or venerated by those who worshiped her thousands of years ago, there is nonetheless much to learn from these ancient tales about the strength and divinity of a powerful female figure like Shapash.

## Qetesh

Qetesh is an ancient Canaanite goddess whose popularity endured for centuries. Translating to 'the Holy One,' her name is rooted in majestic power, and her legends captivate with stories of forbidden love, lustful passion, and hypnotic dance. Today, devotees worship the goddess in rituals that draw from the deep well of symbolism associated with Qetesh, such as snakes, lilies, and mandrakes. Typically worshiped as a mother goddess of fertility, Qetesh holds immense power. She could create life out of chaos by granting knowledge and unlocking new potential. Her strength has been talked about throughout history; many scholars have noted that Qetesh's radiance still beguiles those who seek divine guidance.

## Resheph

Have you ever heard of Resheph, the Canaanite goddess of life and death? She was known as a "runner," whose name possibly means "flame" or "lightning ."Resheph was honored in many ancient mythologies and stories in which she protected the community of Canaanites by taking away sickness and disease as well as punishing wrongdoers. She was viewed as both a protective and corrective force who could choose to take action against injustice. Her worship included offerings of oxen, horses, bread, oil, beer, perfumes, and more. Her symbols were bulls, cedar trees, and burning arrows, with correspondences including sunlight, stars, winter season, and thunder. As an agricultural goddess with a powerful association to fire energy and divine forces, Resheph had a much greater influence than what remains in modern-day records. She was believed to be a warlike goddess who would stand against spiritual and physical enemies, safeguarding her people from harm and danger.

## Tanit

The goddess Tanit was an essential part of Canaanite mythology. Her name is thought to mean "Goddess of the Earth," and she was widely venerated as the Mother Goddess and guardian of fertility. Stories and myths surrounding Tanit included her being the nursemaid to Baal, a powerful fertility deity. Ancient cults were devoted to worshiping her, often with offerings such as bread, fruits, and grains during periods when rain and plentiful harvests were prayed for. Her symbols are related mostly to nature, and she's associated with lunar cycles, depicted in ancient art as a woman wearing a moon crown with horns on either side. Though not always connected with war or battle gods in stories, it's believed her power was vast enough to confer success in difficult times. Ultimately, Tanit was an example of the classic "Earth Mother" type of goddess, much like Gaia and others worldwide who wielded remarkable amounts of power.

Canaanite goddesses are some of ancient mythology's most powerful and mysterious figures. From Shapash's solar might to Qetesh's captivating stories, these powerful female figures can teach us much about their divine strength and the importance they hold in their respective societies. We will never know all of the secrets that lie within these ancient stories, but by learning more about the goddesses of Canaanite mythology, we can gain insight into a fascinating world not far removed from our own. These goddesses are a reminder of the power that femininity can have and how female figures can continue to be symbols of strength and protection in the world today. With that, we can honor their legacy by striving to create a better world for all of us.

# Chapter 5:

## Religious Beliefs and Practices

The Canaanite religion had an incredibly strong influence on the ancient world. Passed down from one generation to the next, its traditions held significant importance to many during this period. The Canaanite culture stretched far and wide in its significance, and its teachings left a long-lasting legacy for centuries to come. As such, it's not surprising to see how it founded the foundation for some of the earlier religious beliefs of today. From ethical codes to moral norms based on justice, there is much evidence showing how elements of Canaanite religion made their way into other societies across the globe. Despite its largely peaceful nature, it certainly left an impression and will likely remain revered in some circles for years to come.

This chapter will focus on the religious beliefs of those following the Canaanite religion. It will discuss how and where they used to worship their deities, what their temples used to look like, and the practices they used to follow. Finally, it will provide an overview of how you can apply these same practices today and the benefits that can come from doing so.

## Religious Beliefs of the Canaanites

The Canaanites were a group of Ancient Semitic-speaking peoples that lived in the Levant region on the Eastern Mediterranean Sea before the rise of Israel. They had an interesting set of religious beliefs and practices that greatly impacted the other civilizations around them, including ancient Greece and Rome. Many scholars believe their beliefs laid a foundation for many major religions, both past and present. Besides the main members of the pantheon, worshipers also believed in other gods, such as Yaw, Anat, and Mot, who represented various aspects of humanity and nature. As such, it can be said that the Canaanite religion laid the framework for understanding complex ideas regarding god, nature, and human relationships with both of these aspects.

## Places of Worship

The Canaanites held their temples in high regard, treasuring them as sacred places to interact with the divine. These places of contact between humanity and the gods were incredibly important, seen as serving both practical and spiritual needs. The worship of gods within these temples provided communal unity, allowing worshippers to meet at a shared physical space to express devotion. Furthermore, many offerings made at these temples served practical requests, such as asking for success in battle or protection from pestilence. Whether honoring the gods or pleading for an individual request, the temple remained a central focus for Canaanite life.

Temples were large and ornate structures built from brick, stone, and mud. They were often decorated with intricate designs in the form of sculptures, paintings, and other artwork. Inside the temple was an altar where sacrifices were made, a shrine to store statues of the gods, and incense burners to fill the air with sweet-smelling smoke. Many of these ancient temples remain standing today, offering a glimpse into the past. Some of these include the temples at Tel Be'er Sheva and Megiddo, both of which offer insight into what the Canaanite religion was once like. Other temples are still used today but in a slightly different way, such as the Church of the Holy Sepulcher in Jerusalem.

## Rituals and Practices

The Canaanites were Near Eastern people who lived in the areas of present-day Syria, Lebanon, and Israel. Before they were conquered by the Israelites around 1200 BCE, they developed many of their unique rituals and practices. Their religious practices primarily revolved around the worship of El, their chief god, as well as his consort Asherah and other deities. Funerary rituals also played an essential role in Canaanite culture.

Archaeological evidence shows that burial offerings such as pottery and jewelry were common in tombs dating back to the Early Bronze Age (3500-2000 BCE). In addition, divination was widely used among the Canaanites to foretell events or gain insight into special circumstances. Although little remains from this fascinating ancient culture today, it is clear from our archaeological discoveries that the Canaanites had a long-standing tradition of ritual and practice, which has since been lost to antiquity.

## Festivals and Celebrations

The Canaanites celebrated many festivals throughout the year in honor of their gods. Sacrifices of animals and food offerings were commonly made at the temples, and feasts were held to commemorate special occasions. These festivals served as important social events where members of the community could come together to show reverence for their deities and gain insight into the future. Some of the festivals celebrated by the Canaanites included Akitu, a spring fertility festival; Zagmuk, a winter solstice celebration; and Ta'anit Ester, a spring festival of thanksgiving.

## Applying Canaanite Practices Today

Applying Canaanite practices today may seem daunting, but with a little research, some determination, and an open mind, it can be quite rewarding. Understanding this ancient culture and its customs provides insight into our ancestor's cultures and traditions as well as unforeseen connections with certain current beliefs. Each era and region of the world has had its unique rituals, so while it is hard to apply all of those in the same way, incorporating pieces here and there can bring positive energy to one's life. Taking the time to learn about these practices will enrich your understanding of Judaism or any other faith stemming from those ancient roots and allow you to move forward confidently in today's ever-changing world.

Here are some tips for applying the Canaanite practices to your life:

- Research the culture and its rituals. This includes reading about various gods, offerings, ritual practices, and festivals.

- Attend religious ceremonies or visit ancient temples when possible. This will give you a firsthand look at the culture and allow you to gain insight into its practices.

- Try to find modern equivalents for the ancient rituals. This can be done by researching how other religions use similar practices or by creating your interpretation of the rituals.

- Don't be afraid to experiment and try new things. Be open-minded to new ideas and try to incorporate them into your daily life.

- Finally, remember that each culture has its own unique beliefs and practices. Don't be discouraged if some of them don't resonate with you as strongly as others.

By exploring and understanding the Canaanite culture and its rituals, you will gain a deeper appreciation for the world around you. In addition, you may find ways to incorporate these ancient practices into your own life, bringing positive energy and insight along the way.

The Canaanite culture was one of the oldest and most influential in ancient Near Eastern history. Understanding their religious beliefs, rituals, and festivals can provide insight into our ancestors' cultures and beliefs. By researching this ancient culture and its rituals, we can find modern equivalents for the various practices and incorporate them into our lives. By doing so, we can gain an appreciation for the world around us and bring positive energy and insight into our own lives.

# Conclusion

The Canaanite religion was deeply connected to their cosmology. It served as a source of understanding for the people and enabled them to make sense of the world around them. The Canaanites believed that the world was made up of three realms: the heavens, the earth, and the underworld. The gods resided in the heavens, the humans and animals lived on earth, and spirits dwelt in the underworld. The gods were seen as powerful yet distant sources of power that could be used to manipulate the natural world.

The gods of Canaanite mythology often interacted with humans, providing guidance and protection in times of trouble while also punishing them when they disobeyed the gods' laws. From El, the ruler of the gods, to Baal and Anat, divine siblings who represented fertility and war, respectively, the Canaanite religion was filled with powerful deities. Canaanite goddesses were equally important to the religion and often acted as intermediaries between the gods and humans. The principal goddess was Asherah, the mother goddess associated with fertility and childbirth. Other important goddesses included Anat, the goddess of war, and Astarte, the goddess of love.

Canaanite religious beliefs and practices were centered on worshiping the gods and goddesses, as well as offering sacrifices to them. Offerings were often made during festivals and religious ceremonies to gain the gods' favor and protection. Religion also played an important role in the everyday lives of the Canaanites, with many participating in rituals such as blessing their crops and seeking the gods' guidance in difficult decisions. Canaanites also believed in life after death and hoped to be reunited with their ancestors in the afterlife.

Overall, the Canaanite religion provided structure and meaning to life for its believers and offered them a way to connect with the gods and goddesses of their mythology. Although the Canaanite religion has largely been lost to time, it still serves as an important source of insight into the beliefs and practices of ancient civilizations.

This book has provided you with an overview of the Canaanite religion, from its history and cosmology to its gods, goddesses, and religious practices. It covered the major aspects of the religion, offering a thorough introduction to this ancient belief system. You should now have a better understanding of the Canaanite religion and its influence on ancient civilizations. While this religion may be extinct, its legacy still lives on in our knowledge and understanding of it.

Canaanite religion was, and still is, an interesting and complex religion with a great deal of variation from one region to another. There's still a wealth of knowledge about the beliefs and practices of this ancient civilization. We hope that you will use this book as a starting point for further exploration. The knowledge you gain will provide you with a deeper understanding of the history and culture of ancient Canaanite civilizations.

# References


Bronze age religion - Canaan & ancient Israel @ university of Pennsylvania museum of archaeology and anthropology. (n.d.). Penn.Museum. https://www.penn.museum/sites/canaan/CanaaniteReligion.html

Canaanite mythology/myth. (n.d.). TV Tropes. https://tvtropes.org/pmwiki/pmwiki.php/Myth/CanaaniteMythology

Nakhai, B. A. (2003). Canaanite Religion. In Near Eastern Archaeology (pp. 343–348). Penn State University Press.

Study of Antiquity and the Middle Ages [@studyofantiquityandthemidd4449]. (2020, November 21). The origins of the ancient Israelite religion | Canaanite religions | mythology. Youtube. https://www.youtube.com/watch?v=zVnQqtYCS_M

The Editors of Encyclopedia Britannica. (2014). Canaanite religion. In Encyclopedia Britannica.

The gods and goddesses of Canaan. (2016, August 20). Raymondusrex. https://raymondusrex.wordpress.com/2016/08/20/the-gods-and-goddesses-of-canaan

www.ingramcontent.com/pod-product-compliance
Lightning Source LLC
Chambersburg PA
CBHW061621130726
47996CB00003B/1081